ANIMALS Are NOT Like US

CATS

For a free color catalog describing Gareth Stevens Publishing's list
of high-quality books and multimedia programs, call 1-800-542-2595
(USA) or 1-800-461-9120 (Canada). Gareth Stevens Publishing's Fax:
(414) 225-0377. See our catalog, too, on the World Wide Web: gsinc.com

Library of Congress Cataloging-in-Publication Data

Meadows, Graham.
    Cats / by Graham Meadows.
      p. cm. — (Animals are not like us)
    Includes bibliographical references and index.
    Summary: Describes the physical characteristics and behavior
of cats, pointing out ways in which they differ from people.
    ISBN 0-8368-2251-X (lib. bdg.)
    1. Cats—Juvenile literature. 2. Cats—Physiology—Juvenile
literature. [1. Cats.] I. Title. II. Series: Meadows, Graham.
Animals are not like us.
SF445.7.M435   1998
636.8—dc21   98-18764

North American edition first published in 1998 by
Gareth Stevens Publishing
1555 North RiverCenter Drive, Suite 201
Milwaukee, WI 53212 USA

Original edition published in 1998 by Scholastic New Zealand Limited,
21, Lady Ruby Drive, East Tamaki, New Zealand. Original © 1998 by
Graham Meadows. End matter © 1998 by Gareth Stevens, Inc.

Printed in the United States of America

1 2 3 4 5 6 7 8 9 02 01 00 99 98

ANIMALS Are NOT Like US

CATS

Graham Meadows

Gareth Stevens Publishing
MILWAUKEE

Cats are not like us.

Cats can see at night much better than we can.

At night, their eyes become big and round so they can see in darkness.

In the daytime, cats' eyes become little slits to keep out the bright light.

Cats are not like us.

Cats can hear better than we can.
They can hear the faint squeaks
made by mice or rats.

Cats' ears are more pointed than ours.

Cats can point their ears forward to hear sounds in front of them.

They can turn their ears backward to hear sounds from behind.

Cats are not like us.

They pick up scents better than us.

They like to stop and smell scents as they walk around.

Cats rub against
things to put
their own scent
on them.

This lets
other cats
know they
are not the
only visitors.

11

Cats are not like us.

They can taste things better than we can.

If their food is not fresh,
they will not eat it.

Cats are not
like us.

They can move
around more
quietly than
we can.

Pads on the bottoms of their feet help them creep up on their prey.

Cats are not like us.

Cats talk to each other in different ways from us.

meow

hiss

growl

They meow, hiss, growl, yowl, chirp, and purr.

16

Cats raise
their fur to
show they
are angry
or frightened.

They raise
their tails to
say "hello."

17

Cats are not like us
at all, are they?

Glossary

angry — upset with someone or something. *Cats sometimes hiss when they are **angry**.*

chirp — a quick, squeaking sound made by certain small animals, such as cats and insects. *A **chirp** is short and high-pitched.*

creep *(v)* — to move slowly with the body close to the ground. *A cat or another animal might **creep** if it is trying to silently sneak up on prey, such as a mouse.*

daytime — during the day, within the hours between dawn and dark. *Cats spend a lot of time sleeping during the **daytime**.*

faint — not clear; dim. *A cat's sense of hearing is so good that it can hear the high, **faint** sounds made by a mouse.*

forward — to or toward the front of something. *Cats can point their ears **forward** to hear sounds in front of them.*

fresh — just made, grown, or served; not old. *Most cats will not eat food that is not **fresh**.*

frightened — afraid; scared. *The fur on a cat's back might stand up straight when it is **frightened**.*

growl — a low, deep, angry sound, sometimes made by an animal that is frightened or upset. *A cat might **growl** if it is frightened by a dog.*

hiss — a sound like a long sssssssssss, such as the noise made by an angry cat. *A cat might **hiss** at another cat to show who is in charge and to scare the other cat away.*

meow — the sound that a cat makes. *A cat **meows** for many reasons, such as to say hello, to be playful, and to indicate hunger and the need for affection.*

pads — the cushions on the feet of a cat. *These **pads** help cats sneak up softly and quietly on their prey.*

pointed — coming to or having a sharpened end. *The lead in a pencil may be either dull or **pointed**. Cats' ears are **pointed**, and they can stand straight up.*

prey — an animal hunted by another animal for food. *A cat that is kept inside might pounce on a real mouse or a toy mouse as though it is **prey**!*

purr — the low, soft, rumbling sound made by a happy cat. *A cat may **purr** when it is being petted or when it is expressing affection for a human or another cat.*

quietly — with little or no noise; silent or almost silent. *Cats have the ability to move around very **quietly**.*

scent — a special smell given off by an animal, person, or object. *Cats like to smell the **scents** around them inside the house or in the yard. They also like to rub against objects to put their own scent on them and to communicate with other cats that visit the same area.*

slits — long, narrow openings or cuts. *The opening in a cat's eye that lets in light becomes a little **slit** during the daytime, when the light is bright.*

squeaks — high, thin cries or sounds. *Cats can hear the faint **squeaks** made by mice and other animals.*

yowl — a loud, howling cry. *Cats sometimes **yowl** when they want to go outside.*

Activities

. . . .

Going Wild!

Find a book in the library that has information about the wild relatives of pet cats — lions, cheetahs, leopards, tigers, jaguars, and others. How are these big, wild cats different from house cats? How are they alike?

A Homemade Cat Toy

You can make a cat toy out of a small rectangle of felt fabric and a piece of thick yarn. Fold the felt in half and draw the outline of a mouse's body on the top layer. Ask an adult to help you cut out the shape, cutting through both layers of felt. Glue the two pieces together with white glue, leaving a small opening near the tail end. Stuff the mouse with cotton balls. If you want, you could also put some catnip in the toy. As you glue the opening closed, add a tail of yarn.

Be a Track Star!

Draw a picture of the pads on a cat's foot. Then ask an adult to cut a potato in half. With a felt-tip marker, draw an outline of the cat pads onto the potato. Ask the adult to carve away all of the potato around the pads you have drawn. Carefully dip your potato stamp into paint and stamp cat tracks on pieces of paper that you can use for gift wrap.

Make a Cat Mask

Cut sections out of the top of a paper plate, so that large, pointed ears are left. Ask an adult to help you cut out eye holes. Then use crayons, markers, pipe cleaners, and scraps of construction paper to add a mouth, nose, and whiskers. Attach elastic thread to both sides of the mask to keep the mask on your face.

Books

Amazing Cats. Alexandra Parsons (Knopf)

Big Cats. Small Cats. Animal Families (series). Markus Kappeler (Gareth Stevens)

Cats. David Alderton (Dorling Kindersley)

Cats. Norman Barrett (Franklin Watts)

Do You Like Cats? Bank Street Ready-To-Read (series). (Gareth Stevens)

Mitzi, Molly, and Max the Kittens. Gisela/Siegfried Buck (Gareth Stevens)

My First Kitten. Rosemarie Hausherr (Four Winds)

My Pet Cat. LeeAnne Engfer (Lerner Publications)

Videos

The Cat. (Barr Films)

The Cat Family. (International Film Bureau)

Dogs, Cats and Rabbits. (Public Media, Inc.)

The Family Chooses a Pet. (Video Dimensions)

Friend for Life. (Pyramid Film & Video)

Just Call Me Kitty. (Unicom)

Kittens to Cats: A Video Guide to Owning the Perfect Cat. (Video Dimensions)

Pets: A First Film. (Phoenix/BFA)

Web Sites

www.catlovers.com

www.bestfriends.org

homepages.ihug.co.nz/~ meadows/animal.htm

Some web sites stay current longer than others. For further web sites, use your search engines to locate the following topics: *cats, kittens, pets,* and *humane society.*

Index

Former veterinarian Graham Meadows is the author and/or photographer of over seventy books for children about animals.

It was while working as a vet at the Aukland Zoo in New Zealand that Graham Meadows's interest in animal photography began. He finds the way animals look and behave endlessly fascinating. His desire to pass on this enthusiasm to a younger generation has led him to produce the *Animals are not like us* series for three- to seven-year-olds.